Create your own

# Luxe Soap

hinkler

# CONTENTS

**hinkler**

Published by Hinkler Books Pty Ltd
45–55 Fairchild Street
Heatherton Victoria 3202 Australia
www.hinkler.com

© Hinkler Books Pty Ltd 2019, 2021

Author: Erin Moeller
Cover Design: Aimee Forde

ISBN: 978 1 4889 2566 5

Printed and bound in China

# INTRODUCTION

Few things are quite as satisfying as being able to enjoy a beautiful, luxe soap. It is not only a practical and essential part of self-care, but the look, feel, scent and texture can bring joy to your senses and soul.

You can elevate this experience even further by creating this sumptuous soap yourself! With the simple but effective melt-and-pour soap-making technique, you can bring the spa experience to everyday life for yourself, your family and friends. So let's get started!

As fun as soap making is, there are certain safety precautions that need to be followed. The soap and container can get hot while melting. Use caution around children and pets. Use pot holders to handle hot containers of soap. Be aware of potential allergies to fragrances and added ingredients when selling your soapy creations or giving them away as gifts.

# ALL ABOUT SOAP MAKING

There are several different soap-making methods. This book focuses on the quickest and easiest approach: melt-and-pour soap making.

## Soap-making Methods

Crafting handmade soap falls into three different soap-making methods: melt-and-pour, cold-process and hot-process.

## Cold- and Hot-process Soap

The classic methods are cold process and hot process. Cold- and hot-process soaps are made by combining oils and fats with sodium hydroxide lye to create a chemical reaction called saponification. Lye is a highly corrosive agent and so making soap these ways involves much more stringent safety precautions. These methods also need much more equipment, and trial and error to design the perfect recipe that will be cleansing without being over-drying. In addition, you need to wait a minimum of 4–6 weeks to cure your finished bars of soap before you can use them.

## What is Melt-and-pour Soap?

Melt-and-pour soap is the easiest and most convenient way to dive into the world of soap making. All the difficult work has been done for you. You begin with cold-process soaps made with sodium hydroxide that have already been cured for you. Melt-and-pour soaps are higher in glycerine, which will naturally leave your skin soft and smooth. The higher glycerine content allows the soap to be easily manipulated without all the fuss of cold-process soap.

Just cut up your soap, put it into a heat-safe container, and slowly melt it either in the microwave or in a double boiler (see more details on these methods on page 7). Create your own handmade soaps for yourself or to give away as gifts, all without the stress of working with sodium hydroxide.

# GETTING STARTED

This section will go through the fundamentals of melt-and-pour soap making, including the materials involved, safety precautions and some useful general tips and techniques that will prepare you for making the most successful luxe soaps.

## Materials for Making Melt-and-pour Soap

### Essential Materials that Come with the Kit

#### White Soap Base

The white soap base supplied in the kit is very easy to work with. It can be melted and reused as often as you need. It makes the art of soap making simple and satisfying – even for total beginners!

White soap is a great plain base for creating a pastel palette of colours. The soap base will work well with any added scents or textures you wish to add. The options are endless!

#### Soap Moulds

There are four lovely soap moulds ready to use in this kit! They will help you create stunning handmade soaps. They are made from firm plastic, which is easy to get soap in and out of as you learn and they also allow for a variety of different shapes.

You can source extra moulds for your soap making through craft stores and online. You could even look for fun and unique shapes in your supermarket's baking section or a specialist baking shop.

Silicone moulds are another great option and are very popular for soap making. They're easily available from many soap retailers and are a breeze to clean. One of my favourite moulds is the 10.16cm (4-inch) silicone loaf mould. The full interior measurements of the mould I use is 6.66cm (2 5/8-inch) height x 8.90cm (3 1/2-inch) width x 10.16cm (4-inch) length. It makes a traditional bar soap that you cut to the width you prefer.

#### Pipette

Pipettes are really useful for soap making. They can be used to add scents and colours, for colour mixing, and for adding colour layers to soaps.

If you decide to use fragrance oils for your soap, you definitely need a pipette to measure the oils precisely. Just make sure you clean the pipette out thoroughly after use to avoid mixing scents.

If you're working with a soap mould with an intricate design, pipettes are a great way to ensure that you're getting the melted soap into every detail. You can even cut the pipette a little to make the opening larger if needed.

#### Stirring Stick

You will need some sort of utensil for mixing ingredients, colours and fragrances into your soaps. It is also useful for helping melt down the soap consistently if you are melting it over a stovetop or cooker. You can use a standard stainless steel spoon, a rubber spatula, or even a craft or popsicle stick!

The wooden stick supplied with the kit is heat-resistant and should be used for soap making only.

### Other Useful Soap-making Materials

#### Other Soap Bases

Melt-and-pour soap bases come in many varieties and are readily available at craft stores, speciality soap stores, or online. Many soap bases come with luxury ingredients like shea butter and olive oil, which are moisturising for your skin. Another popular option is a clear soap base. This can be particularly useful if you want to suspend ingredients such as flowers, soap embeds (other pieces of coloured soap), toys, or even to demonstrate multiple colours within your soap.

Keep in mind, though, the clearer the soap base, the higher the glycerine content. This means it will be more likely to 'sweat' or collect beads of glycerine on the surface of the finished soap if it's left out too long. To avoid this process, make sure to wrap up your finished soap in cling wrap until you're ready to use it.

## Rubbing Alcohol

A spray bottle of rubbing alcohol is extremely useful in melt-and-pour soap making. A quick spritz onto your layers will pop any stray bubbles that have formed. This will give your luxe soaps a more professional appearance.

If you're making a layered soap, a quick spray between the layers of soap will also help the layers adhere better. You won't have any fear of the layers separating!

## Natural Additives

There are so many natural ingredients that you can incorporate into your luxe soaps. These additives can add colours, textures, scents and benefits for the skin when the soap is used. Many common pantry and fridge items can be used, from milk to carrots!

Some popular additives are honey, colloidal oatmeal (finely milled and pressed whole-oat kernels), activated charcoal, natural clays, flowers, and coffee and tea. We will go through using some classic ingredients, like coffee and honey, in the projects in this book.

**WARNING:** Ensure that ingredients you add to your soap are clean, cosmetic-safe, and their use-by dates are clear.

## Essential Oils

If you want to keep your soap as natural as possible, essential oils are a wonderful way to add fragrance to your soaps. Essential oils are usually made by distilling a natural source, such as a flower, and retain the scent of this source, and sometimes other therapeutic benefits, such as nutrients.

Some popular essential oils for soap making are lavender, chamomile, lemongrass and tea tree.

**WARNING:** Bear in mind that some essential oils are not recommended for use on skin, so familiarise yourself with safety instructions for each oil you are considering. Buying essential oils from a soap-making shop is a good way to obtain information about their safe use.

## Synthetic Additives

There are also a wide range of manufactured additives you can add to your soaps for different effects, looks, scents and textures.

### Colourants

You can get liquid colourants that have been pre-dispersed in glycerine, powdered mica or even glitters! As well as adding colour, many synthetic glitters and mica colourants add texture to your soaps.

## Scale

In this book, soap is measured out by the gram (with conversions to ounces provided). You don't need to invest in an expensive scientific scale; a standard kitchen scale that measures to the nearest gram or ounces rounded to the nearest two decimal places will do. The soap in this kit is in 75-gram (2.65-ounce) blocks.

## Measuring Bowls, Cups and Spoons

I recommend a heat-resistant measuring bowl or cup to weigh out and melt your soap. Microwave-safe glass is the material I recommend as I always melt my soap in the microwave. But you can just as easily use a heat-safe bowl to melt it over the stove. You will also need measuring spoons to measure any added ingredients.

## Thermometer

Measuring the temperature of your soap will be necessary for certain techniques in melt-and-pour soap, such as the optimal temperature to add fragrance. My favourite tool is an infrared thermometer. However, when you get started, a kitchen thermometer will do just fine!

**WARNING:** Do not use candle dye or food colouring to colour your soaps. It is important to use only colourants that are certified as safe to be in contact with skin.

### Fragrance

Fragrance oils are synthetic ingredients that can help achieve a luxury scent for your soaps. You can find many store and online suppliers for fragrance oils – buy the best quality ones you can, and always check the safety usage for soap making for each particular brand and type of oil that you use.

**WARNING:** Some people have fragrance allergies or sensitivities, so use caution when adding these, and ensure that the recipient is aware of all the ingredients.

### Other Utensils

### Protective Wear

Melt-and-pour soap is the safest way to create beautiful, usable works of art. However, you still need to be cautious of the hot melted wax, during the melting, pouring and setting stage, as it can burn the skin.

**WARNING:** Use potholders or oven mitts while handling containers of melted soap.

Don't leave hot liquids unattended where children or pets can reach them.

If you're selling or giving your luxe soaps to family or friends, I also recommend wearing disposable medical gloves as you create your soaps to ensure hygiene.

Just make sure you remember to clean it thoroughly before using it for cooking – or better yet, keep one dedicated to your soap making.

## Knife and Cutting Board

You will need a sharp, non-serrated knife and cutting board to cut the soap base to get the correct amount. If you choose to use a loaf mould to craft your soap, you will also need this knife to cut your soap into the final luxe bars to share.

## *How to Melt Soap*

The soap should melt at around 50–70°C (122–158°F). It depends on what soap base you use. The glycerine in the kit will start melting at around 68°C (154.4°F).

• Since microwaves can come with different wattages, you may have to experiment with the melting time. I recommend doing a practice run first. Start with shorter bursts of 15–30 seconds for the initial melting, and go down to 5–10 second bursts after the soap has melted a little. You don't want to overheat your soap as it will affect the finished product.

• Overheated or burnt soap will become cloudy, and will have a thick, unworkable texture. If your soap boils, it is definitely considered burnt. It will likely have an unpleasant smell. There really is no way to save the soap at this point. It's best to toss it out and start again.

• You can also use either the double boiler or slow cooker/rice cooker methods, if you prefer. The slow cooker/rice cooker methods are a great way to keep your soap at a consistent temperature without the need to reheat.

• To use the double boiler method, simply bring a pot with roughly 2.5–5 cm (1–2 inches) of water to a boil. Reduce to a simmer, and place your heat-safe container with cubed soap into the pot. Slowly melt the soap until the desired temperature is reached. Glass will work best with this method – be sure to use a pot holder as the container of soap will get hot!

• You can also use a rice cooker or slow cooker to melt your soap. Place cubed soap into cooker. If using a slow cooker, set to high. If using a rice cooker, set to white-rice setting. Keep an eye on the soap as it melts. As soon as the soap is at the right temperature, reduce the heat setting. This method works best if you're making a larger batch of soap. You may not want to use this method unless the slow cooker or rice cooker is dedicated to soap making.

• Ideally, fragrances should be added under 80°C (176–180°F). Heating your soap beyond this may reduce the strength of your fragrance – particularly with essential oils.

# LAVENDER AND LACE SOAP

*The Lavender and Lace Soap is a beautiful, classic bar of soap. Using the soap mould with the lace-latticed pattern that comes with the kit will accentuate the elegance of this soap.*

## You will need:

- 100 grams (3.53 oz) of white melt-and-pour soap base (cut and weighed with kitchen scale)
- Heat-safe container to melt soap (needs to hold 200 ml/ 7 fl oz or more)
- Thermometer
- Lavender floral buds
- Soap-mixing stick
- Lace soap mould from the kit

## Optional:

- 1.5 ml (0.05 fl oz) of fragrance of choice (You could use lavender to enhance the scent of the natural lavender buds or a complementary scent such as rose.)
- Pipette
- Rubbing alcohol in spray bottle

*1.* Place 100 grams (3.53 oz) of white melt-and-pour soap base into a heat-safe container. Melt in the microwave using short 10–15 second bursts until it is liquid.

*2.* If you like, add lavender essential oil or lavender fragrance oil. Then, if the soap is beginning to cool too quickly, microwave it in 10–15 second bursts until it's workable. Adding in fragrance cools the soap slightly, so reheating ensures the mixture remains easy to pour.

### Handy Hint:

If adding fresh botanicals to your soap, allow the soap to thicken slightly before pouring. That way the botanicals won't sink to the bottom of the soap.

*3.* Pour one layer of the white soap onto the lace patterned mould. This layer should just be thin enough to cover some of the lace detail.

*4.* Add the lavender floral buds. Stir in gently to avoid adding too many air bubbles into the soap base. You can choose to spray the tops of the soap with rubbing alcohol to pop any bubbles.

**5.** After the buds have been well incorporated, pour into the lace mould. You can spray rubbing alcohol onto the first layer before pouring the second layer of soap to help the layers adhere. Let the soap sit at least 3 hours before removing the soap from the mould. You now have the perfect lacey accessory to any bathroom – why not impress by saving some for yourself as guest soaps?

## Handy Hint:

Lavender is known for its calming and soothing benefits. It is also well known for its purifying and cleansing properties. If you use pure lavender essential oil, you will keep this soap as close to nature as possible. If that's too expensive, you can use lavender fragrance oil instead. You could also crumble up some clean, fresh lavender if you wanted!

# LUXE LAYERED OMBRE SOAP

*A simply stunning bar of soap! The eucalyptus and spearmint fragrance goes perfectly with the ombré soap layers that range from white to a pale teal.*

## You will need:

- 565 grams (20 oz) of white melt-and-pour soap base (cut and weighed with kitchen scale)
- Heat-safe container to melt soap (needs to hold 750 ml/ 26.4 fl oz or more)
- Thermometer
- Soap-mixing stick
- Loaf soap mould
- 1/4 teaspoon of turquoise or mint-green colourant total (this will be distributed among all layers of the soap)
- Ruler
- Large knife
- 4.5 ml (0.16 fl oz) of eucalyptus essential oil or fragrance oil
- 4.5 ml (0.16 fl oz) of spearmint essential oil or fragrance oil
- Pipette
- Optional:
- Fresh spearmint leaves and/or eucalyptus leaves
- Rubbing alcohol in spray bottle

1. Place 565 grams (20 oz) of white melt-and-pour soap base into a heat-safe container. Melt in the microwave using short 10–15 second bursts until liquid.

2. If you like, now would be the time to add the fragrances. Carefully measure using the pipette and stir gently. You can also choose to use, or substitute fresh leaves. If the soap is beginning to cool too fast, microwave in 10–15 second bursts until it's workable. Adding in fragrance cools the soap slightly, so reheating ensures the mixture remains easy to pour.

3. Pour a small portion of white soap into the loaf soap mould. This will create the first layer. Spray with rubbing alcohol to pop any bubbles.

4. For the remaining layers you will slowly add the colourant to the remaining white soap. You can make as many or as few layers as you like, just adding a little bit of the 1/4 teaspoon of colourant into the remaining soap for each layer. The colour will get more vibrant with each addition. Gently mix this in, re-melting the soap base if necessary. When the soap in the mould is solid to the touch (usually within 10 minutes depending on the layer thickness), spray with

rubbing alcohol to adhere the layers together. Pour a portion of the soap base into the mould to create the next layer. Spray with rubbing alcohol to pop any bubbles and allow to cool until slightly hardened. Follow this with a layer of the clear soap base. This layer needs to be thinner, but eyeballing the amount is fine. Spray with rubbing alcohol and allow to cool.

### Handy Hint:

If you want very even layers, you can put your soap mould on your scale and weigh each layer as you pour until they are even. You can have fun with intentionally doing differently sized layers, though!

5. Repeat steps 3 and 4 until all layers are created. Add a little colour to the liquid base each time, and pour layers onto the solidified soap in the mould. Spray the top of the final layer of soap with rubbing alcohol to pop any remaining bubbles. Allow the soap to cool at least 3 hours, or ideally overnight, so it completely solidifies.

6. Cut the soap loaf into bars. The easiest way to get consistent-sized bars is to measure them with a ruler. Using your knife, cut small notches into the soap; then using a large knife apply even pressure to slice all the way through the soap in one smooth motion. The soap may stick to the blade. If so, carefully twist the soap off the knife. And there you have it, a beautiful and refreshing bar to enliven any shower or bath experience.

# LA VIE EN ROSE SOAP

*This delightful bar of soap celebrates the classic rose and will help you retain a rosy complexion.*

## You will need:

- 75 grams (2.65 oz) of white melt-and-pour soap base (cut and weighed with kitchen scale)
- Heat-safe container to melt soap (needs to hold 200 ml/ 7 fl oz or more)
- Thermometer
- 1 teaspoon of rose clay (this can be found with the natural colourants and clays in a soap supply store)
- 1 tablespoon rubbing alcohol
- Soap-mixing stick
- Circular soap mould
- Rubbing alcohol in spray bottle
- Dried rosebuds for decoration

## Optional:

- 1 ml (0.03 fl oz) of fragrance of choice (There are many different varieties of rose fragrance available, or you could use a different floral fragrance.)
- Disposable pipette

1. Place 75 grams (2.65 oz) of white melt-and-pour soap base into a heat-safe container. Melt in the microwave using short 10–15 second bursts until liquid.

2. Prepare the rose clay for colouring the soap. Combine 1 teaspoon of rose clay with 1 tablespoon of rubbing alcohol. Blend until smooth. Pour the clay–alcohol mixture into the liquid soap until the ideal colour is achieved. You might not use all the clay mixture.

### Handy Hint:

The rose clay used in this soap is not only a great colourant, but is also helpful for soothing dry or inflamed skin.

3. If you like, you can add a fragrance of your choice. If the soap is beginning to cool too fast, microwave in 10–15 second bursts until it's workable. Adding in fragrance cools the soap slightly, so reheating ensures the mixture remains easy to pour.

### Handy Hint:

A fun variation of this soap is to use clear glycerine soap. You can add rose petals instead of buds and have them suspended in the clear base.

**4.** After all the ingredients have been well incorporated, pour into the soap mould. Spray the top of the soap with rubbing alcohol to avoid bubbles. Allow the soap to cool slightly before adding the rosebud decorations. The soaps need to be slightly thickened so that the rosebuds don't sink to the bottom. Allow to cool for at least 3 hours before removing from the mould. A small dried rosebud adds a beautiful decoration to this rose clay soap. This is the perfect nurturing gift for someone special – their skin will feel as gorgeous as a bed of roses.

## Handy Hint:

If you want very even layers, you can put your soap mould on your scale and weigh each layer as you pour until they are even. You can have fun with intentionally doing differently sized layers, though!

# WAKE UP! COFFEE BEAN SOAP

*The gentle scrubbing sensation of the natural coffee grounds in this soap will leave skin feeling fresh and smooth, and the coffee scent is the perfect energiser.*

## You will need:

- 75 grams (2.65 oz) of white melt-and-pour soap base (cut and weighed with kitchen scale)
- Heat-safe container to melt soap (needs to hold 200 ml/7 fl oz or more)
- Thermometer
- Soap-mixing stick
- 1/2 teaspoon of coffee grounds
- Square soap mould
- Rubbing alcohol in spray bottle
- Whole coffee beans for decoration

## Optional:

- 1 ml (0.03 fl oz) of fragrance of choice (You could use a coffee fragrance to intensify the coffee goodness, or a complementary fragrance, such as vanilla.)
- Disposable pipette

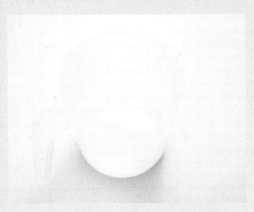

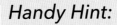

**1.** Place 75 grams (2.65 oz) of white melt-and-pour soap base into a heat-safe container. Melt in the microwave using short 10–15 second bursts until liquid. The soap should melt at around 50 degrees Celsius (122°F).

**2.** Gently blend in the 1/2 teaspoon of coffee grounds. If the soap begins to solidify, you can reheat in the microwave in 10–15 second bursts.

### Handy Hint:

You can use either fresh coffee grounds or repurpose used grounds from your morning's coffee. Fresh grounds may add more colour to your soap, though and are less likely to be contaminated!

**3.** After you have blended in the coffee grounds, you have the option to add in a fragrance if you like. If the soap is beginning to cool too fast, microwave in 10–15 second bursts until it's workable. Adding in fragrance cools the soap slightly, so reheating ensures the mixture remains easy to pour.

4. After the coffee grounds and fragrance have been well incorporated, pour the soap into the mould. Spray the top with rubbing alcohol to pop any air bubbles.

5. Add coffee beans on top for decoration after the soap starts to cool slightly. (If the soap is too hot, the beans will sink.) Gently push the beans into the soap surface so they are partly submerged and less likely to fall off. Allow the soap to cool in the moulds for at least 3 hours before you remove them. You now have the perfect way to get energised for your day!

# SUPERB CHARCOAL SWIRLS SOAP

*The technique used in this project swirls together several colours of melt-and-pour soap. The addition of activated charcoal ensures this soap gives a deep clean while being gentle on your skin.*

## You will need:

- 570 grams (20.11 oz) of white melt-and-pour soap base (cut and weighed with kitchen scale)
- 3 heat-safe containers to melt soap (need to hold 250 ml/ 8.8 fl oz or more each)
- Thermometer
- Soap-mixing stick
- 1/4 teaspoon of activated charcoal
- Blue liquid soap colourant (or soap colourant of choice)
- 6–9 ml (0.21–0.32 fl oz) of sandalwood essential oil or fragrance oil
- Disposable pipette
- Loaf soap mould
- 3 separators for soap mould
- Popsicle stick, chopstick or similar mixing tool
- Rubbing alcohol in spray bottle
- Optional:
- Small amount of turmeric or cinnamon spice.

1. Divide the white melt-and-pour soap base into thirds so that there is 190 grams (6.7 oz) in each of the 3 heat-safe containers. Melt in the microwave using short 10–15 second bursts until liquid. Melt all soap at once so all colours remain around the same temperature.

2. Gently blend in 1/4 teaspoon of activated charcoal into one container, and your colourant of choice in another. I used a liquid glycerine soap colourant and used a few drops at a time to reach the desired colour. If the soap begins to solidify, you can reheat in the microwave in 10–15 second bursts.

3. Add the sandalwood fragrance using the pipette and stir gently. If the soap is beginning to cool too fast, microwave in 10–15 second bursts until it's workable. Adding in fragrance cools the soap slightly, so reheating ensures the mixture remains easy to pour.

4. Place the separators into the soap mould. You can buy pre-made ones, or make them yourself from cardboard or up-cycled materials. Pour a different-coloured soap into each separate section. You need to work quickly and carefully so the soap doesn't begin to cool too fast.

### Handy Hint:
The key to making good swirls is to simply run the popsicle stick around a couple times, and then stop, however tempting it might be to keep stirring. Too much swirling will spoil the desired effect.

**5.** After all the soap has been placed into the sections, remove the separators. Carefully swirl the sections together with a popsicle stick, chopstick or similar tool.

**6.** If you like, add a spice to the top of the soap as it cools to add fragrance and texture. Allow the soap to cool at least 3 hours to fully solidify. After it is completely cooled, cut the soap into bars. You now have a beautiful whirlpool piece of soap art!

# STAINED GLASS SOAP

*This Stained Glass bar of soap is a showstopper! Using clear melt-and-pour soap between the layers of colour allows you to see through the bar of soap, creating the effect of a stained-glass window.*

## You will need:

- 424 grams (14.96 oz) of white melt-and-pour soap base (cut and weighed with kitchen scale)
- 285 grams (10 oz) of clear melt-and-pour soap base (cut and weighed with kitchen scale)
- 3 heat-safe containers to melt soap (need to hold 350 ml/12.32 fl oz or more each)
- Thermometer
- Soap-mixing stick
- 2 x 1/4 teaspoons of soap-safe mica (in 2 desired colours)
- 1/8 teaspoon eco friendly glitter
- Loaf soap mould
- Rubbing alcohol in spray bottle

1. Divide the 424 grams (14.96 oz) of white melt-and-pour soap base evenly into 2 heat-safe containers (212 grams/7.48 oz in each). Place 285 grams (10 oz) of clear melt-and-pour soap base into the remaining heat-safe container. Melt in the microwave using short 10–15 second bursts until liquid.

2. Gently blend 1/4 teaspoon of the first colour of soap-safe mica into one of the white soap-base containers until the desired colour level is reached. Gently blend the second colour into the other white soap-base container. If the soap begins to solidify, reheat in the microwave in 10–15 second bursts.

3. If you like, add a fragrance of your choice. Simply split the fragrance between the three containers of melted soap base. If the soap is beginning to cool too fast, microwave in 10–15 second bursts until it's workable. Adding in fragrance cools the soap slightly, so reheating ensures the mixture remains easy to pour.

4. Place the mould on a base, like a book, so one side is angled higher than the other. Pour the first layer of coloured soap to the level you'd like. Spray with rubbing alcohol to pop any bubbles and cool until slightly hardened. Follow with a thin layer of the clear soap base (eyeballing the amount is fine). Spray with rubbing alcohol and allow to cool.

**5.** Next, rotate the soap mould so that the angle is going the opposite way. Pour a layer of the other coloured soap base. Spray with rubbing alcohol and allow to cool and slightly harden. Follow with a layer of the clear soap base. Spray with rubbing alcohol and allow to cool until slightly hardened.

**6.** Repeat steps 4 and 5 until the mould is full, re-melting the soap base as needed in 10–15 second bursts.

**7.** Allow the soap to cool at least 3 hours to completely solidify. After it is completely cooled, cut the soap into bars.
Once you have perfected these windows, try experimenting with different colours and thicknesses. Maybe you can even add a third one! Just make sure to remember to always put the clear layer between each coloured layer.

## Handy Hint

Allow each layer to cool until it is slightly firm to the touch before adding the next layer. This will result in clean lines. Don't rush it! You can always re-melt the soap.

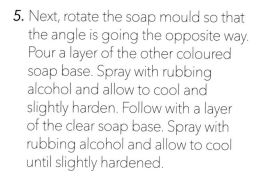

# BEE MY HONEY SOAP

*The Bee My Honey soap is easy to make and looks boutique with your beehive mould! We recommend that you add soothing and luxurious natural honey and colloidal oatmeal to bring the soap to the next level.*

## You will need:

- 75 grams (2.65 oz) of white melt-and-pour soap base (cut and weighed with kitchen scale)
- Heat-safe container to melt soap (needs to hold 200 ml/ 7 fl oz or more)
- Thermometer
- Soap-mixing stick
- 1/2 teaspoon of colloidal oatmeal
- Rubbing alcohol in spray bottle
- 1/8 teaspoon honey
- Bee soap mould

## Optional:

- 1 ml (0.03 fl oz) of fragrance of choice, such as Oatmeal, Milk & Honey fragrance oil
- Disposable pipette

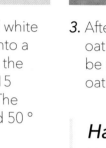

1. Place 75 grams (2.65 oz) of white melt-and-pour soap base into a heat-safe container. Melt in the microwave using short 10–15 second bursts until liquid. The soap should melt at around 50 ° Celsius (122°F).

2. Gently blend in the colloidal oatmeal. Sometimes the oatmeal doesn't blend in well, but just be patient and work it in the best you can. Spray with rubbing alcohol to pop any air pockets. If the soap begins to solidify, reheat in the microwave in 10–15 second bursts.

3. After you have blended in the oatmeal, add in the honey. This will be easier to incorporate than the oatmeal.

### Handy Hint

You can also make your own colloidal oatmeal! If you have rolled oats at home, you can grind it down to a fine powder using a food processor, blender, or a spice grinder!

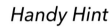

**4.** If you like, add a fragrance of your choice. If the soap is beginning to cool too fast, microwave in 10–15 second bursts until it's workable. Adding in fragrance cools the soap slightly, so reheating ensures the mixture remains easy to pour.

**5.** After all the ingredients have been mixed, pour the mixture into the bee mould. Let it sit at least 3 hours before trying to remove your soaps. You will be buzzing with good health and vitality in no time!

### Handy Hint

Colloidal oatmeal consists of finely milled and pressed whole oat kernels. It's an ingredient used in skin care for its soothing properties, including relieving itchy skin and sunburn. Honey is a natural humectant, meaning it adds moisture to your skin.

# AMETHYST GEODE SOAP

*This soap is sure to impress everyone! It looks like a beautiful crystal stone, and is the perfect sculptural artwork for your bathroom.*

## You will need:

- 605 grams (21.34 oz) of clear melt-and-pour soap base (cut and weighed with kitchen scale)
- 100 grams (3.53 oz) of white melt-and-pour soap base (cut and weighed with kitchen scale)
- Heat-safe container to melt soap (needs to hold 600 ml/ 21.12 fl oz or more)
- Thermometer
- Purple soap-safe colourant
- Soap-mixing stick
- Loaf soap mould
- 1/4 teaspoon eco-friendly glitter
- Chopstick or popsicle stick
- Rubbing alcohol in spray bottle
- Cutting board
- Large knife

## Optional:

- 9 ml (0.32 fl oz) of fragrance of choice (Some blends are inspired by gemstones, or use a light, floral fragrance!)
- Disposable pipette

1. Place 180 grams (6.35 oz) of clear melt-and-pour soap base into a heat-safe container. Melt in the microwave using short 10–15 second bursts until liquid. Add the purple soap-safe colourant and mix until the desired amethyst colour is achieved. Add in 2.5 ml (0.09 fl oz) of fragrance if desired, re-melting if necessary. Pour into the soap mould and allow it to become slightly firm.

2. Place 425 grams (15 oz) of clear melt-and-pour soap base into a heat-safe container. Melt in the microwave using short 10–15 second bursts. Add 1/4 teaspoon of eco-friendly glitter. Add 5.5 ml (0.19 fl oz) of fragrance. Pour into the soap mould on top of the purple layer. Break through some of the layers using a chopstick or popsicle stick to achieve a more natural, less straight crystal colouration.

3. Place 100 grams (3.53 oz) of white melt-and-pour soap base into a heat-safe container. Melt in the microwave using short 10–15 second bursts. Add 1 ml (0.04 fl oz) of fragrance if desired and pour into the soap mould. Break up the layers slightly with a stick. Don't go down too deep; just break the line between the clear and white layers. Spray the top with rubbing alcohol to pop any bubbles. Allow to cool for at least 3 hours so the soap fully hardens before cutting.

4. The cutting of this soap creates the crystal shape. You can achieve 4 large crystals, 16 smaller crystal spikes, or a combination of both. If you would like to make the larger crystals, cut the loaf in half. For smaller crystal spikes, cut 4 even slices.

5. For larger crystals, cut the soap slices in half again to make 4 pieces. For smaller spikes, cut the slices into another 4 equal slices to make 16 pieces.

6. Next, on all of the crystals, cut the corners off the soap. Make sure that dark purple is on the bottom and white is on the top.

## Handy Hint:

The key to this project is the way the soap is cut. Don't obsess about perfection, though. Very few natural crystals look perfectly symmetrical. An imperfect shape will give this soap a natural crystal look. And you can reuse the discarded soap! Simply place the soap pieces into a batch of melted soap base to create a confetti-inspired soap that kids will love!

7. Carefully cut into the corners of the deep purple end until the desired shape is formed. That's it! Now you have beautiful crystal soap! Make more in different colours and create your own bathroom crystal cave.

# CONGRATULATIONS!

You have started on your journey of creating your own luxe handmade soap! Now you've mastered the basic techniques of melt-and-pour soap making, you can take these skills and make your own unique soaps. It is very addictive – there are endless combinations of colours, fragrances, looks and textures. The beautiful thing about handmade soap is that it's something you can use every day to add brightness and happiness to your life. And if you run out, just make more!

Be sure to look around online to explore more of the wonderful world of soap making. There are so many handmade soap artisans out there that you can share your delightful creations with and be inspired by. Keep sharing and finding new ways to make this lovely art form your own. Combine techniques and soap bases, colours and textures. I can't wait to see what you create!

# MEET THE AUTHOR!

Erin Moeller lives and works on her soapy creations in the northern suburbs of Chicago. She's a self-taught soap artisan, and she loves to find new ways to add creativity to the art of soap. When she's not elbows-deep in soap making, she's playing with her little boys, running her Etsy shop, or doodling in one of her many sketchbooks.